The Circle of Illusion

The Circle of Illusion

Poems by

Gurcharan Rampuri

Translated from the Punjabi by
Amritjit Singh and Judy Ray

With a Preface by Amritjit Singh

for Bob
welcome
aboard)
Amritjit
sept 28,
2012

چ چ چ
Weavers Press
San Francisco, California

Some of the poems in this collection have previously appeared (some in variant forms) in the following publications:

Chelsea: "The Circle of Illusion," "Let This Home Begin to Think Again," "Peace Song: A Duet," "Rampur"

Edinburgh Review: "Pens Coming Together," "Distinction" (previously entitled "Recognition"), "The Whip"

Kavya Bharati: "The Courtesan," "The Primal Act Leads to Beauty," "Rest," "Sleep," "The Twentieth Century"

Mascara Literary Review: "2 Ghazals," "Opportunists," "Pet Lies," "Today"

New Letters: "Burn Down the Old Tree," "Word and Horns"

Nimrod: "We Are Lost in Our Own Village"

Re-Markings: "Advice," "Blind Alley," "The Stake"

Salzburg Poetry Review: "The Embrace," "The Moon Lifts the Night"

South Asian Ensemble: "Before We Meet," "Doe-Eyed," "An Entreaty for Canada," "Moments," "The Monsoon Cloudlet"

South Asian Review: "Let Us Walk in Unexplored Woods," "The Moment of Creation," "My Wool," "Dividing Line," "Loneliness," "Your Letter Has Not Come"

Toronto Review: "Faith," "Massacre," "Phoenix," "Song of the Stream," "Spring"

All poems have been translated by Amritjit Singh with Judy Ray, with the following exceptions which are also indicated in the text:
Poems on pages 20-21, 23, 35, 54-55, 72, and 75 are translated by Amritjit Singh with Wendy Barker; poems on pages 36 and 37 are translated by Amritjit Singh with Georgia Scott.

Cover painting: "Mother Earth" by Arpana Caur, used with gracious permission of the artist   www.arpanacaur.com
Cover design: Wendy Goldfarb
Book design: Judy Ray

ISBN: 978-0-9843776-0-2

Weavers Press
San Francisco
http://weaverspress.wordpress.com

To my wife
Surjit Kaur
(1935-2003)
who shared her life and love with me
for 53 years

CONTENTS

Preface

Gurcharan Rampuri has been writing in Punjabi for well over sixty years and has lived in Vancouver, BC, since 1964. Born in Punjab, India, in 1929, Rampuri worked for eight years as a draftsman with the Punjab Government Electricity Board before he migrated with his family to Canada. While I did not meet him in person until 1988 during a visit to Vancouver, I had heard about him in the 1950s when I was a young boy growing up in Ambala. I would often see his poems in Punjabi magazines and also hear about him from my father, who was a professor of Punjabi literature, and from the late Surjit Rampuri, Gurcharan's childhood friend and "poetic" twin. As their shared *nom de plume* suggests, Surjit and Gurcharan grew up in the village of Rampur, near Doraha (literally, "a fork in the road"), situated mid-way between Ludhiana and Khanna. In Rampur, the two boys took long walks by the Sirhind Canal and talked late into the summer nights about girls, poetry and politics.

Rampuri gave his first public reading in 1946 and has since 1953 published ten volumes of poetry – all in Punjabi. He has also edited a few anthologies of Punjabi poetry. His *Collected Poems* appeared in India in 2001. Many of his lyrical poems have been set to music, sung by well-known singers like Surinder Kaur and Jagjit Zirvi, and made available on cassette. His poems have been translated into many languages, including Russian, Urdu, Hindi, and Gujarati. A volume of his Punjabi poems, *Sanjha Asman* (Shared Sky) was published in Pakistan in Persian script (*Shahmukhi*), the preferred script for Pakistani Punjabi writers.

In Vancouver – in 1988 and again a year later – I was impressed by the passionate personal style of Gurcharan Rampuri, a tall handsome man with a powerful voice. During my two visits, I met many Punjabi writers of Indian and

Pakistani background. I was fortunate to experience directly the sense of community these diasporic writers were struggling to maintain against the pull of their own strong personalities, their immigrant lives fractured by race and distance from their native language and culture, as well as the clashing ideologies in both British Columbia and back home in the Punjab. For example, after the tragic events of the 1980s and 1990s in Amritsar, New Delhi, and elsewhere, whose aftershocks continue to be felt in the life and politics of the Punjab and in the Punjabi communities around the globe, Rampuri and a few other writers felt compelled to respond to the fault lines that surfaced in the Punjabi/Sikh population of Vancouver, the largest anywhere outside of the Punjab.

In this volume, we present a cross-section of Rampuri's poetic oeuvre that I hope conveys its range and complexity. I have translated most of these poems over many years with my poet-friend Judy Ray of Tucson, Arizona. As indicated in the text, six poems were translated with poet Wendy Barker of San Antonio, Texas, and two others with poet Georgia Scott, an expatriate American who lives and teaches in Gdánsk, Poland.

The poems included here are not "transcreations," as defined by Kolkata poet, P. Lal, or poems inspired by the original poems in Punjabi. As translators, we have worked assiduously to stay close to the original text even as we have aimed at making a poem in modern English. As the native speaker of Punjabi, I would first prepare a line-by-line, stanza-by-stanza translation of each poem and consult with the poet mostly by phone as often as necessary. Then, my co-translator and I would begin our work together to turn that detailed first translation – through a minimum of three or four intervening drafts – into the final product. For their attentive engagement in this process and for their faith in the end result, I owe a deep debt of gratitude to Judy Ray, Wendy Barker, and Georgia Scott. Also, artist Arpana Caur of New Delhi graciously gave permission for us to use her painting, "Mother India," which resonates so well with many of Rampuri's motifs in his poetry. Thanks, Arpana.

In this book you will come across poems from different periods of Rampuri's literary life, reflecting the diversity and complexity of his themes and interests. We have included many lyrics and love poems, as well as a few that many readers would regard as political. But most of the work included here strikes a meditative or philosophical note. Even the personal and political poems are often reflective in their affect, and Rampuri is at his best when questioning the orthodoxies of attitude and belief.

I asked Rampuri once in a phone conversation about his relationship as a young poet to the Left-leaning Progressive Writers Movement, whose meetings he used to attend in the 1940s and 1950s. "Just as I have moved in form from the demands of metered verse to the liberating territory of 'free verse' and *doha* (rhymed couplet), I have also journeyed in other ways from faith to doubt," he responded. Not unlike writers, such as Richard Wright, Ignazio Silone, and Arthur Koestler, whose disillusionment with Communism is anthologized in Richard Crossman's *The God That Failed* (1949), Rampuri began in the 1950s to view Communism as a dogma that restricts individual freedoms and full artistic expression. Over the phone, he recited one of his couplets:

> *Jeebh jandré soch sunn bhala naan oh parbandh,*
> *rété uté hai khari eh pathar di kandh.*
> (Any regime that places locks on tongues and benumbs
>   thinking
> Is like a wall standing on foundations of sand.)

Rampuri tells me that today he has zero tolerance for any dictators or ideologies – whether from the Right or the

Left. His poetry reflects the complex, broad-minded humanism that he has shaped out of his experiences in both India and Canada. The poem "The Moment of Creation" suggests the challenges of capturing the inspired moment in words. Rampuri tells me he often feels better prepared to meet that challenge in a quiet room of his own – undistracted by work, money, or pettiness. While rhyme and meter are not always part of his verse today, rhythm is still an essential element. He sees no reason why his free verse as well as his lyrics might not be sung. Among various forms, Rampuri has practiced the *ghazal*, a form of amatory verse where each rhymed couplet is a complete unit in itself conveying a distinct feeling or situation or mystical truth about unrequited love.

At 82, Rampuri seems more than satisfied with the attention and acknowledgment he has received as a poet, both in India and abroad. But I find it amazing that a poet of his maturity and vision has lived in North America for over forty-five years, yet is barely known to literate Canadians or Americans. I hope this volume of his poems will introduce readers to the range and depth of his poetry, and to his versatile uses of language and image.

Ohio University   *Amritjit Singh*

A word from the poet...

I started writing poems in 1944 when I was barely 15. Maybe we are all poets in our teen years; some put their thoughts on the page, others don't.

The 1940s were an eventful period of modern history. In 1944, World War II and India's freedom movement were both entering a decisive phase. My earliest poems were inspired by the prospects of India's freedom from colonialism and surrounding tensions.

World War II was won by the allied forces and at least for once fascism was defeated. Negotiations for India's freedom intensified. The arrival of freedom was bittersweet. India was divided into two nations along religious lines. Hundreds of thousands were butchered, millions uprooted from their ancestral homes. I saw human beings' brutality to those of other faiths, but many fought against this insanity and sheltered their neighbors from mindless violence. Mahatma Gandhi brought the violence in and around Calcutta to an end through his fasting. These tragic circumstances deeply affected me and my poetry.

My poetry has given me a purposeful life. I have received little royalty money for my publications. But many individuals in India and Canada who have known me only as a poet have assisted in my need for gainful employment to provide bread for me and my family.

I have been fortunate to have enjoyed the community of fellow writers throughout my life – for example, Progressive Writers Union and other literary associations in India, as well as the Writers Union of Canada based in Toronto and the Punjabi Literary Forum, Vancouver. When asked, I have served in leadership roles in these societies, but mostly I have benefited intellectually and spiritually from my friendships with many writers, including some well-known figures.

I am grateful to Amritjit Singh and Judy Ray, Wendy Barker and Georgia Scott, for their special attention to my work as translators and interpreters. I hope their labor of love will allow some of my poems to reach a wider audience.

This volume is dedicated to my late wife, Surjit, who allowed me to steal some of her time for poetry for over five decades. I also owe a debt of gratitude to all my children for their caring love in my advancing years: Devinder and Manjit, Harmo, Jas and Kal, Rav and Cheryl. In 2006, the doctors and nurses at the Royal Columbian and Queens Park Hospitals in Westminster, B.C., brought me back from the *door of death* to the *shore of life*. I salute them all with this volume!

Coquitlam, B.C., Canada   *Gurcharan Rampuri*

The Circle of Illusion

ਰਾਮਪੁਰ

ਪਿੰਡ ਮੇਰੇ ਕਵਿਤਾ ਜੰਮਦੀ ਹੈ
ਮਹਿਕ, ਮੁਸਕਣੀ, ਮਿੱਟੀ ਦਾ ਮੋਹ, ਮਿਹਨਤ, ਮੁਸ਼ਕਾ
ਰੂਪ ਰੰਗ ਕਟਕਾਂ ਤੇ ਕੁੜੀਆਂ
ਚਹਿਕ, ਚਾਨਣੀ, ਅੰਬਰੂ ਵਿਚ ਆਕਾਸ਼ ਉਤਰਿਆ
ਕੰਡਿਆਂ ਦੇ ਲੰਗਾਰਾਂ ਵਿਚ ਵਹੀਟਾਂ ਦੀ ਚਾਂਦੀ
ਅੱਗ, ਨਿੱਘ, ਰੋਸੇ ਦੀ ਠੰਡਕ
ਬੇਦਲੀਲ ਵਿਸ਼ਵਾਸ ਅਨੇਕਾਂ!

ਬੇ-ਮਿਸਾਲ ਇਹ ਪਿੰਡ
ਧਰਤ ਦੇ ਹਰ ਪਿੰਡ ਵਰਗਾ
ਜਾਗਾਂ ਰਹੀ ਉਡੀਕ ਇਹਨੂੰ ਵੀ ਕਿਸੇ ਕਲਮ ਦੀ।

ਪਰਸ ਅਨੇਕਾਂ ਕਲਮਾਂ ਦੀ ਕਦ ਛੋਹਾਂ ਮਰੀਆਂ ?
ਮੋਹ ਦੀ ਤ੍ਰਿਪਤੀ ਕਦੋਂ ਹੋਈ ਹੈ ?
ਇੱਕ ਨੋਕ ਤੇ ਸਾਰੀ ਸੁੰਦਰਤਾ ਕਦ ਸਿਮਟ ਸਕੀ ਹੈ ?

رامپور

پنڈ میرے کوتا جندی ہ
مہک، مسکنی بنی دا مینہ محنت مڑھکا
روپ رنگ کٹکاں تے کڑیاں
چہک چانڻی امبرو وچ آکاش اتریا
کنڈھیاں دے لنگاراں وچ وہیٹاں دی چاندی
اگ نگھ روسے دی ٹھنڈک
بے دلیل وشواس انیکاں

بے مثال ایہہ پنڈ
دھرت دے ہر پنڈ وانگوں
یگاں رہی اڈیک ایہوں دی کسے قلم دی

پرس انیکاں قلماں دی کد چھکھاں مریاں؟
موہ دی ترپتی کدوں ہوئی ہے؟
اک نوک تے ساری سندرتا کد سمٹ سکی ہے؟

16

Rampur

The birthplace of poetry is my village –
its fragrant aromas and smiles,
its devotion to the land, hard work and sweat,
its swaying beauties and fields of wheat,
its merriment, moonlight, and tears reflecting the sky,
the silvered waters curving the banks of the canal,
the warmth of bonfires, coldness of lovers' quarrels,
and its many illogical beliefs.

My village is unique,
yet just like any other village in the world
it has waited centuries for a poet's pen.

Even the work of many pens will not satisfy its longing.
Who is ever content with the gift of affection?
How can such loveliness rest only on the nib of one pen?

Words and Horns

When the word was born
the horns disappeared.
But when we turn our back upon the word
animal rage rises again.

Before you leap across a chasm,
pause and take stock of your strength.
Your head may be in the sky
but keep your feet firmly on the ground.

When you slip from the collar of logic,
poison pervades your mind.
Blind rage and reason
are ancient enemies.

You, not those strangers or neighbors,
are the root of your own troubles.
Within you lies
the cause of your pain.

Take off those horns from your head
and rediscover the word.
The healing nectar is within.
Seek it within yourself.

Pens Coming Together

I
Waves converge to raise the storm.
All the blossoms spread their fragrance.

II
When the strings are touched, music soars
with inspired harmonies to intoxicate the soul.

III
Atoms gather to fashion the universe
and drops of water collect to become the sea.

IV
Rays of the morning sun compose songs.
And when pens unite, they change history.

Phoenix

The mind flounders in an ocean of doubts,
swims, dives, and surfaces again.
Dives in search of pearls.
Swims to get somewhere.
Surfaces to balance, look around,
get out of the self and speak.

Truth and doubt – twin
brothers through the ages,
eternal rivals.

Old truth won't balance the scales.
My cheating stares in my face
when I try to tip the balance in yesterday's favor
and I am ashamed.

Why can't someone make it easy
by blindfolding me?
I vacillate like the prophet Abraham,
weighing his son's life against God's word.

My fellow travelers are bitter that
I am no longer swayed by the mantra.
But I can't stop questioning myself:
Why give up the comfort of the trance?
Why must I lift the rock to the mountain top?
Why take on the sifting desert sands?
Why relish the flames so close?

If yesterday's truth doesn't measure up,
how can we trust today's?

How can I yield to the past
that just sits there, a worn-out courtesan?

Once again the phoenix is gathering
sticks and straw for its pyre.
For the dance of a new life
it snaps the thread of its own breath
to stage its death.

Translated by Amritjit Singh and Wendy Barker

Sleep

Sleep is like a woman –
When you invite her, she declines.
When you try to banish her
she lays her palms on your eyes.
And when she does arrive
she floods your heart with dreams.

When sleep stays for only a fleeting time
it leaves you so racked,
as if with sharp shards of truth and lies,
you cannot even wring your hands.

Song of the Stream

Listen to the mountain stream's
music, the run of life

that moves with machine-age speed
but nurtures no grudges,
skips with grace over rocks,
rounding their edges.

Listen, listen to this music
that holds a million chimes
and the drums of war.

Listen to the sounds of its feet
carry the vows of lovers
and their restless waitings.

On its banks shivers a cool virgin scent
causing a quiver
with its own warmth.

Sun-sparked falls crash onto rocks
noisy as a feisty wife complaining.

Come sit with me by the rainbow's
spray of life.
Why run back to the smog and crowds of the city?

Translated by Amritjit Singh and Wendy Barker

The Primal Act Leads to Beauty

When I first met her
I knew she was the one I had been searching for.
I had found my dream
and my aimless quest had at last found purpose.

She saw me, drew back in fear, then smiled.
Covering the secret centers of her body, she blushed.
My eyes lingered on her striking beauty
and in my turmoil I lost my bearings.
Neither of us knew the right words
yet somehow we found them.
Our hands touched first, then our lips,
and then we were as one in a love embrace.
I was in her and she had entered
every pore of my being.
Lightning exploded in the sky
leaving us dazzled by its brightness.

As if enjoying a carnival in the middle of a forest,
I had a wild time with her.
There were butterflies hovering all around
and birds in their courtship dance.
With our coming together in love and joy of life,
with color, warmth and closeness conjuring the creation of
            beauty,
I felt surrounded by peace, reveling in fragrance and light,
her rosy, glowing skin,
the experience of a repeated miracle.

Then the priests and holy men arrived
and these fools began to preach about beginnings and ends.
With their mumbo-jumbo tales

these nincompoops delivered unwanted sermons.
They told me, You have been ensnared by the Snake,
by Satan, and tangled in poisonous vines.
Your actions have angered God,
and you stand expelled from paradise.

And this was my reply to them:
I need no intercession to justify
my union with the beautiful one.
I have stolen no one's fortune.
I am surrounded by heaven, which I embrace.
As for this delectable primal act
which creates life and beauty –
how can anyone call it a sin?

The Courtesan

Always we have been told:
Why does the obvious need to be proved?
Yet all truths come to light
on pedestals of doubt.

The rising and setting of both moon and sun are lies.
The blue bowl of the sky above our heads
is an illusion, too.
Those stars, sparkling like pinholes of light,
are greater than a million earths together.
Flowers weep, and stones writhe.
Even within the ocean an immense fire may burn.

A person proclaiming human rights
may inside be an ugly Hitler.

We have traveled to the moon and back
but have yet to overcome boundaries between nations.

Politics, Religion, Civilization –
these all resemble the courtesan's smile.
But how can she who is for sale be trusted?

Burn Down the Old Tree

The old tree, stricken and useless,
has wide crevices,
a golden nest of snakes.

Every day pet crows drop a few stolen coins
into the tree's hollows.
The hoarded gold dies.

Those coins do not turn into bread
but become a poisonous weight.
That gold does not nurture the tree's roots.
As poison seeps into each of its veins,
its disease advances.
Don't plead any more for its recovery –
Just burn it down!
Free the captive gold, converting it to wages, to bread.
Bring an end to this hunger the whole village suffers,
bring warmth into its cold life.

From the womb of the tree's ashes a satin shoot will smile,
new branches stretch into the sky.
Once again the season of blossoms will swell.
Once again woods and clearing will fill with fragrance.

Helen Keller

Helen Keller (1880-1968), deaf and blind from infancy, learned the concept of words and the ability to speak from her teacher, Anne Sullivan. Keller became a scholar and author, traveling throughout the world as a representative of the American Foundation of the Blind.

Your courage is the rising sun
that conquers all challenges.
Your words
are those of Adam and Eve when they first met,
of love at first sight.

Your vision is unique in its bearing.
In your heart lives the whole world.
Your heart has imagined the beloved
and created a land of love.

You felt Adam's face with your hands.
Your tongue, your eyes, your ears are all asleep
yet your imagination flames with fire.

Every cell in your body enjoys the song.
Your hands speak for you.

Roses bloom in your mind
appealing for color, scent, and smiles.
Even without light of sight
you give them radiance and luster.
In your garden, the roses blossom and beam.
In your garden is perpetual spring.
Autumn never enters there.

In your world, rivers flow
and your hands feel the warm currents.

You too must have wept and wiped tears from your eyes.

Your dreams
must be transcendent.
I wonder how you might have created an image of radiance
how in your heaven lamp and candles get lit
how the sun and stars burn
how the moon shines
how the birds sing
how the mother's love flows into lullabies
how someone's daughter smiles.

You converse with heavenly kisses.
No talk is distant.
The ritual of your hands defines intimacy.
In your world there are no false promises, only empathy and
        love.
Even a strand of hair responds to the gentlest touch.
Talk is pointless.

You have created an ocean of hope,
a lust for life.
You are an icon of struggle,
confronting fate without fear.

God exiled Adam from paradise
but humans can yet turn this world into heaven.
Today life strives against failings.

The rock of foretold fate is slowly eroding.
You are great, you are the ray of life!

Strangers

for Native Canadians

They are the original owners of this land,
theirs is the story the artist tells.

I narrate the centuries
that are older than history,
larger than millennia.

It was when the land was a huge glacier
or a brutal, merciless jungle
that these brave people
came here in their struggle for life.

These pure, guileless souls
for whom feathers are crowns
and nature's multicolored
grandeur is a source of joy
live a life of song and dance
amidst frost and stony frozen silence.

They sculpt beauty from rock
and for them bone is needle, surgeon's knife,
artifact, and weapon too.

In the wars for survival
they have won many a battle.
These hard-working, proud
souls did not even feel a need for God.

Then one evening the white skin arrived as a guest
bringing cunning, liquor, guns,

disease, God, and begging bowl.
Their honor and joyful dance were stolen from them.

Even the name of their land
was taken away from these heirs of the earth.
And then their confident smiles disappeared,
never to return to innocent lips.
Today they are strangers lost in their own home.

But this drunk
gives an occasional knowing glance
and once in a while
he still leaps to the dance.

An Entreaty for Canada

Don't draw a line in the sand, my friend!
Don't draw a line on the land.

Listen to me, please,
lend me your ear.
I come from a land stung by a line
drawn by others a long time ago.
I am a widow whose family was butchered by the line.
I am a lover whose beloved
was abducted and raped by the line.
I am an orphan whose parents were murdered by the line.

A line is venom incarnate
and seals the fate of folks
who realize too late.
A line in the sand becomes a sky-high wall of hate.
How millions suffer I can't narrate.

A line is death and destruction,
tears and homelessness,
a cancer with no cure.
I have already suffered this cancer of the heart.

It doesn't allow a quick death.
It kills you every moment till eternity.

I slipped away from that cancerous line decades ago.
Don't draw a line through my new home.
Don't draw a line, my friend!

Written by the poet directly in English

Let This Home Begin to Think Again

Isn't this home a bit too noisy?

Here reason sleeps and chronic angers reign.
Everyone shouts but no one listens.

Let us get this home thinking again,
let it learn to be silent,
to meditate,
and to reject the posturing of power
as it begins to embrace truth.
Let this home open the third eye
and look inward as do the wise.
Let its members dive deep to find pearls
that lie at the bottom of the ocean of words.

When this home is able to hear the whisper
of a breeze caressing young green leaves,
then will flowers bloom again in our lives,
and the long night of the innocents' suffering will end.

Loneliness

Your indifference and this moonlight –
my thorn-filled garden in spring.
Even in this full-moon night I am in lonely darkness.
My solitary heart longs to meet you again.

I wish I could – like you – forget
all those dreams of being together.
I wish I could pretend I have never played a love song's melody
nor ever known the temptations of love.

You were never mine, nor I yours.
But passion does not honor such reality.
Can the mountains block out the moon?
Then how can anyone hold back the heart's flight?

How can I recount what has happened to time?
How many years have passed since we met?
Who was that couple
who could not bear to be apart even for one second?

Spring

I have your message
to wait a bit longer,
to have patience
before I can ride the crest.

But how could I tell the spring
not to come?
How could I tell the waves
not to crash their heads on the sand?

All I've got is
this one little spring.

Those who want sea-storms to end
before they launch their boats
often never leave the shore.

Why not begin the music that we must sing?
How can we count even on "today"?
It might be gone the next moment.

Translated by Amritjit Singh and Wendy Barker

The Embrace

The longer the embrace
the thirstier the soul.
In this one-of-a-kind bar
even as more glasses are drained
love's euphoria slides
hour by hour.

Even with a topped up drink in hand
reality tastes bitter.
After the gaiety and abandon,
the next moment is bland,
the next hour empty.
Despite those lips' sweet offerings,
the magnificent heat of surrender,
and the imploring eyes
that define the world for me,
I live with fear
of the loneliness that awaits me around the corner.

There's just one way to satisfy the soul –
drink from birth till death,
and live life fully to still the cravings.

Just as the *chakori* bird, dazed with love,
reaches for the impossible moon,
we too surrender to the promise of illusory skies.
But gazing at a stream of stars does not gratify us.
The craving for love is endless.

Translated by Amritjit Singh and Georgia Scott

chakori or *chukar*: the South Asian partridge – regarded as a symbol of unrequited
love – is believed to be fascinated with the moon and always trying to reach it.

The Moon Lifts the Night

You are back at last, my queen,
back again with your smile.

Once more my eyes hold dreams,
my darkness turns to light.
Once again my evenings
color crimson.
Why do others burn so
beneath your moonlit smiles?

When like a sweet melody
you turned away from
the desire
you had kindled in me,
my heart trembled
like a string.
Yet, you threw a glance, like hope,
a smile flashing from your eyes.

One moment you wear a veil of anger,
then you look indifferent,
then you laugh heartily.
What an accomplished actress you are!
Your eyes tell tales without words
and I hear every musical note.
With the miracle of your sudden return
my eyes have become my ears.

You have fallen like a shower
upon the deserts of our separation
smiling, my queen!
Translated by Amritjit Singh and Georgia Scott

Blind Alley

After a few drinks
I consider my score card –
what have I accomplished in my life?

After my schooling, for some years
I climbed the mountain tracks of struggle for my land.
With a sudden turn,
I abandoned these slogans
and became a slave to work,
though I did not put down my pen.

Devotion to beauty outshone my mother-love.
I lost myself in creative work.
I found a partner and loved her,
but I did not forget my joy in the paths I had renounced.
Even the need for bread cannot eclipse the sun.

Money seduced me.
I crossed the seas in search of riches.
But is gold everything?

How wide are the rifts!
The fire of love for family, beauty, and light burns on in me
while mammon's jealous eye tolerates no other smoldering.
Can the flames be kept hidden?
I am trapped in a blind alley.

After a few drinks
we try to tally our scores –
what have we accomplished in our lives?

But then,
after a few drinks
how can we possibly answer this challenge?

Song

In a night of dreams
someone sings sweet songs
She seduces me with
her siren song

Someone knocks time and again
on the door of my soul
In my two wide-awake eyes
she hangs a hundred desires

Waves rise in the lake
like children dancing
Someone leads my longings
the way one would lead a child

Folks are drowsy though the night is young
Moonlight rains down
as someone enters my heart's dark corners
like a beam of light

In the garden of my soul
I hear the footsteps of spring
To whom am I indebted for
the new soft green leaves?

Someone has entered the valley of my heart
like the morning breeze
The shy bud of my soul
opens with each moment

There is a hint in the air that my sleeping life
will blossom into splendor

as moonlight lifts the veil
from its own face

Just as the dawn embraces
the earth each morning
who is it that pervades
my imagination like the sky?

The Whip

I lived for years
under foreign skies
as if I was in my homeland.
I shared the same foods, language, and customs,
the same love, friends, and hunger.
Everything seemed familiar.

Suddenly, there came a moment
when a simple-minded man
lashed me with the whip of a racial slur.
I had been oblivious to reality.
Now I am part of the world that struggles against hate.

Opportunists

Yesterday's friends are today's foes.
Even a brother has a sinister look about him.
Now he accuses with stinging words.
Blood relationships are meaningless.
Today, venomous arrows, daggers, poniards, lances
are plunged into the hearts of one's own.

Yesterday's enemies are in close embrace today.
With wounds from the sword healed,
these sycophants ignore the poison of hate in their hearts
as they dance to the pipes of self-interest,
kiss and lick each other.

Labels pinned on one person yesterday
are now used for another.
Those who were called corrupt
are now held to be virtuous.
It is easy to line up arguments
to justify any good or bad deeds.

Since the dead will not return,
who will want to lose today's profit for their sake?
In pursuing a dream of ideals,
who will ignore the weight of power?
Who will sacrifice national interests
and ignore the lines that divide communities?

Who can beat these sharp villains in glib debate?
So what if they commit awful deeds?

We Are Lost in Our Own Village

The carnival teemed with colors, dreams and trust.
Every moment felt fresh as morning.
Even in the dark we talked of sunshine.
We believed that there at the next turn,
beyond that little wall of time,
lay miracles.
We sought the musk of prosperity,
and in a daze we danced through the nights.

Those miracles of the past –
what have they done for us?
Behind thick walls
we have imprisoned ourselves.
Even when a friend calls out, we don't lift the latch.

The morning paper is full of black-bordered news of funerals.
Who knows if the one who leaves home will return?
Today the eyes no longer mirror the heart.
Friends attack one another at the same time
and both fools die believing themselves victors.

Today's false prophets
feed their secret Swiss accounts.
But they live like rats
and die in the streets, coffinless.
My people yearn for simple colors
as they suffer this hell.
We are lost in our own village.

Doe-Eyed

You are still absent, doe-eyed one!

Hours have passed minute by minute
My spirit has faced many a crisis
as if each moment stopped for a year
My soul has been thirsting for you from the beginning of time

My arms are like an open door
Come to me like the warm western breeze
Without you the buds
will never smile into flowers

I have as many desires as the stars in the sky
Like my longing heart, those stars too gave up hope
One by one they fell asleep
And then came dawn, smiling like you

Come, smile like buds bursting open
Come, turn thorns into flowers
Come, bring life to my feelings
as the sun would make love to the earth

The Monsoon Cloudlet

You came
like a monsoon cloudlet.

My heart burned with separation
hot as a desert.
Passions rose
and a lush life flourished in my soul.
Dreams awakened,
roses sprang up in the wilderness
and a myriad desires blossomed.

Pearls shone in your lap,
hanging like my hopes.
At a hint from you, these pearls
will bring golden glow to my life.
Your bounty will rain upon me,
filling to the brim my empty bowl.
Life will burst into fragrance.

But the storm rages, dejection is deep
and the heart-bird has lost its way.
How can it reach its destination
for even in the lap of light
it endures the dark night?

Lost in a forest of thoughts
I catch the straws of old promises.
I would like to invite you –
to show you the city of my heart.

With a gust of Time
you left as replete as you came
like a monsoon cloudlet
that passed over my courtyard, my sky.
I wonder which town you will rain on.

Rest

My friend the psychiatrist examined me
and sat me down for a chat.
He gave me a shot –
that is all I remember.

Hours later, when I woke up in another room,
the psychiatrist's friendly smile
surely lifted my spirits.

After a few minutes
a beautiful nurse came and said,
"Would you like a coffee, please?"

Then she touched the most tender spot
when she gently asked,
"Why were you crying like a baby?"

"But how would you know?" she went on.
"You were in some far-off place of dreams.
I know artists are emotional people
but it seemed you were in some cavern of distress.
I'm sorry you had to go through so much pain
and the value of your art has not been recognized."

I listened speechless,
wondering what secrets I had blurted out.

She said, "Don't worry. There are still
some in the world who value art.
Art is not a counterfeit coin, after all."

In the evening my doctor friend came again.

Smiling, he reassured me.
"No damage done. But
you need complete rest. You must not
be disturbed by even the slightest
contact with thought."
I said to myself –
that should be easy enough.

I lay down on the blue bed,
relaxed my limbs, and closed my eyes.
And then I saw thousands of figures:
my family praying for my health
even though for them
my art had provided no bread or nice clothes,
and my admirers and critics
whose costly praise brought no returns.

And yes, I also saw those other friends –
who needs enemies with them at your side?

Waking, I wonder if she knows,
she whose teasing glances and subtle smiles
were suddenly withdrawn
and brought me to this state,
she the cruel one –
does she know what misery I am in?

Why do I think at all?
Am I not forbidden to think?
My illness requires complete rest,
with "Do Not Disturb"
to ban thoughts from entering the door.

Before We Meet

I am going to meet someone
but Time is shackled.
My journey seems endless.
Time does not advance by even a second.
It is as if its wings were chained to a mountain.

My imagination runs faster than Time.
In a flash it meets her and returns,
but there is no one home.
Seeing the empty nest, it flies
again to be near her.

A thorn wounds every part of my body.
Loneliness overwhelms me
like the late hours
of a dark, wintry night.

But my dejection is like the morning lamp
that will burn itself out.
A face will smile and light up my eyes.
Then I will wish someone could shackle Time,
add the weight of the Himalayas to its wings
and hinder its flight,
since I am going to meet someone special.

Ghazal

Love smiles when it stumbles.
A star shines throughout its fall.

It takes an age to numb just one pain.
The next moment awakens another hundred.

How can one sleep when longing for the absent one,
And who will sleep on the night of love?

Sadness is my only companion.
Who would befriend me in my melancholy?

The peacocks cry even as they dance.
The swan sings even as it dies.

Beauty yearns for love
as surely as the moon goes around the earth.

One thought contains the universe.
The moon illumines a dewdrop.

Ghazal

I have just burned your letters.
Look, I have bathed in the fire!

Through this pilgrimage to the grave of love
I have revived forgotten pains.

The smooth dark night of your hair –
my fingers have caressed its lush shadows.

I have spent a tearful night
and the dawn is red-eyed.

I have consoled my weeping heart
by imagining scenes of intimacy.

The stars want an encore
though I am done telling my tale.

Life is both sorrow and music,
and I just sang your song.

To light up a glimpse of you in my dreams
I extinguish my own lamp.

Songs, Promises, Tears, Hopes
have won over my estranged lover.

Your Letter

Still no letter from you.
The sun is sad,
and the dim dawn
has not adorned
her forehead with vermilion.

My disappointment hangs heavy, like a thick fog.
The lamp of hope sputters out.
I have waited another long day.
But who has measured the rays of the pole star?
Even as the darkest night cannot hide the stars
so the gloom of sadness cannot eclipse my love's radiance.

Flower petals feel dry –
no dew has come from the sky.
Clouds gather, but not as ambassadors of rain.
These cloudlets carry only empty bags.
What am I to do with the intense colors of flowers?
My morning is without color
since your letter has not come.

Massacre

*for Punjabi poet Ahmed Salim of Pakistan who protested the
1971 tragedy in East Pakistan, now Bangladesh*

That other slaughter happened
before I had words.
Every spot of red was blood.
I couldn't tell apart the mothers lying dead
from the ones who were still alive.
I suckled from both.

Those talkers had mastered gab,
knew how to fake words,
could make you believe a moonless night was noon.
Driven by their power-greed
they fed a poison language to the people.
Sheltered by the enemy's coats
they sliced apart the chest of India,
knifed a line between Ganga and Chenab.
They drowned in the flood of their own slogans,
left the country with open wounds.

Hundreds of thousands dead.
Adam: a statistic.
Eve: a childless widow.

We began over.
People retrieved the kites that had fallen,
and in the spring, let out the strings again.
But the poison had filled the breeze,
the festering sky still filled with shards,
the land riven with ulcers of division.

Across the ocean, the weapons dealers
shed reptile tears, chuckled in their shirts,
relished their profits.

It has happened again. Sudden.
Sons of demagogues have sprung up,
this time neither subtle nor glib,
so proud of the Genghis Khan blood that runs in their arteries
they speak with the tongues of bayonets,
teeth sunk into the flesh of their own people,
death pressed into the land of songs.
Cries thicken the jungle
until Adam's conscience numbs
and vultures, glutted, fly off.

A poet's voice pushes through:
"Stop the butchery.
You will never erase a people.
Those fresh heads you planted
sprout into new guerrillas.
How do you think you bankrupts can do in Bengal
what your financier could not in Viet Nam?"

Fighting over senseless divisions,
Adam's children hear no cries,
their pens shackled,
their brains flooded with blood,
until time
stills the brutality, dissolves all lines.

Translated by Amritjit Singh and Wendy Barker

"That other slaughter" (line 1) refers to the 1947 partition of British India into India
and Pakistan.

Pet Lies

Lies, lies, lies all the time, repeated
until they become today's truth.

A lie sits in the seat of power,
lies are armed with daggers,
lies have many followers.

The platform sure is crowded, in thick fog,
with the confused old holy man in command at the center.
A deafening racket blasts all around
and dark clouds of ruthless death
overshadow the skies.

Brutality, rage, fear and helplessness prevail,
but we cannot escape the need for food.
The terrifying abyss of need has deepened.
Death lies in ambush at every corner.

There is someone walking toward me,
but I don't know if he is friend or foe.
Should I trust his smile, or is it poison?
I will not make eye contact with him,
weighed down as I am by guilt
of sins I didn't commit.

These cheats and cowardly braggarts
keep on throwing dust in the people's eyes,
leading them on with deceitful, well-rehearsed lies.

Professional politicians on the one hand
and the ruling elite on the other,
together they have built their empire of lies.

Distinction

I am the last soldier to die in the war,
O my enemy! O my friend!

In the last minutes of battle
why did your dagger have to plunge into me
at the exact moment
I was dreaming of lying beside my beloved?

Just wait and you will see –
Tomorrow these same leaders, your commanders and mine,
will sit together over drinks
They will smile and divide among themselves
the ground irrigated by our blood.

I am a guest now for only a few minutes.
Be careful, don't set your foot
on a landmine hidden below
because that explosive
makes no distinction between "us" and "them."

Peace Song: A Duet

Fly the flag of peace, my man,
Fly the flag of peace.

Sing a song of peace, my love,
Sing a song of peace.

Who is it that threatens our delight in flowers
with an atom bomb, my man?
Who is it that wishes he could
wither our wombs, my man?

Is he the one who wants to rob
children of their smiles, my love?
Isn't he the one who hastens autumn
for humanity, my love?

The bird's breast throbs as it sings
songs of peace,
yet someone would cage this bird,
hang it by the noose, my love!

With voracious greed for gold,
for strings of pearls and diamonds,
who is the one setting fire
to our folk dances, my man?

Who is the one so zealous
to destroy our silky fields of swaying wheat?
Who enjoys sending our young beauties
into houses of hell, my love?

This warmonger,
enemy of humanity,
wants to dominate the world,
only to loot and exploit, my love.

Wailing widows, mothers, sisters
who lose their men to war,
curse this enemy of love,
compassion and harmony, my man.

Open, searching minds
become dark caverns,
and nibs of pens are broken
at this hawk's command, my love!

But now the defenders of peace have risen.
Amidst green spears of grain, the dove sings,
and we all proclaim,
"No more wars, my comrades!"

Fly the flag of peace,
Sing a song of peace, my love!

The Twentieth Century

The century in which I was born
has also been my father's coeval,
and it is like my father.
This century too is caught in the claws of time.

Just as that eagle called time swooped down on my father
and carried him away,
this century too will fall asleep
after a few winter nights of
indulging in parties and pleasure.

This century that is my father's peer
will hold a salient place in human history.
With one foot trapped in the stone age,
it steps with the other into the open skies of the space age.
A tiny, invisible atom
guided it past the stars.

While some in this century have mapped the heavens for
          humanity,
others remain blind.
They will not waste even a smile on their fellow human beings
and, suffering hell themselves, they are intent upon pushing
          others into hell.

This century lays one hand on the saints' holy shoulders,
but finds its other arm being tugged by demons.
In the midst of this tension,
this century, my mother, radiates a generous smile
as I wait to see where and how it will end.

Future

In the web of calculations
how could it be my fate to find gold?
The wealth-line on my palm is faint.

What kind of future might I foresee?
Will it be suffocated
by the smoke of cars, bombs, and blind faith?

I stole some time from writing poetry
and offered that time before the wolf of greed.
Now that wolf will neither consume it nor let it go
as his angry red eyes stare at me.

If I don't free my time from the wolf
and offer it again to words,
I will be the next victim.
The wolf will swallow me whole.

Today

Yesterday was bearing
a dream called Today.

Revolutionary fervor for the dream
powered a restless sleep.

The enchanting dream
smiled like a golden dawn.

The cursed mother committed
a horrendous crime, killed the newborn dream.
Then with a wild laugh
she went alone and buried the baby.

Yesterday bore Today,
but Today also had a dream which the mother killed.
Now the stunned, murderous soul
stares at the empty space.

Ghazal

Lovers following their destiny get lured into burning paths
They embrace blistering coals like soft velvet

The holy man in deep meditation for thousands of years
is shaken to the core in a minute by beauty's jingling bells

Your indifference healed my sorrow of separation
as if one difficulty resolved another

Don't be complacent, O sailors, as you watch the gentle waves
The surface calm of oceans hides myriad tempests

Sunshine days and dark nights without you are meaningless
And yet I dream of extravagant carnivals in the desert

Advice

Even the smallest peacock feather
holds a rainbow's dazzling glory.
Each fragrance is unique,
and no butterfly is like another.

Through the ages the heart has been called
the Kaaba, holy place of pilgrimage.
Don't pick a flower.
Don't catch a butterfly.
And don't strangle any yearning of the heart.

But who am I to give you this advice?
My child broke a glass
and just now I scolded him.

Kaaba or *Ka'bah*: the holiest site in Islam, a cube-shaped building in Mecca, Saudi Arabia, with a mosque built around it, the Masjid al-Haram. It is associated with daily prayers and the Hajj pilgrimage required of all Muslims at least once in a lifetime.

The Stake

Time and again I visit familiar places.
Time and again I meet the same faces.
Daily, as a devotee, I chant
repetitive verses that no longer speak to me.
My chosen faith will last a lifetime.

Even in the woods
I carved out a new path.
Then I became a prisoner of that track.
Tethered to a stake, I feel so safe.

The Circle of Illusion

The bullock thinks
it is he who powers the oil press,
he who controls the pressed mustard,
he who extracts oil from each seed.
He thinks that his strength moves time,
that each step takes him closer to his destination,
that the music of the oil press plays only for him,
that the bells ring only for his pleasure.

Weary and bathed in sweat,
with his eyes open even in deep darkness,
the bullock thinks as he trudges on:
What though I have blinkers on my eyes –
I have light within me.
What though my path is so long –
still I do not stumble,
and my "servant," the oil man, feeds me fodder.

There is no match for the circle of illusion.
The fevered mind has no dearth of delusion.

Let Us Walk in Unexplored Woods

Our daily routines
make us numb with habit
or is numbness itself a habit?

In habit we will not discover the epic poem
nor dazzling beauty of light
nor heavenly bliss.
Habit is no better than sleepwalking,
just a meaningless dream.

Now and then we should pinch our lovers or ourselves.
Now and then we should stride out with eyes wide open.
Why not walk in unexplored woods?
Then we would savor the ambient scent of fresh flowers.

A few stolen kisses and embraces,
the thunder of uncompromised convictions
could bring us fans from among both friends and foes.

One who is slave to the familiar cannot forge new ways
but even a roundabout route can lead to the goal.
A frame's straight lines seldom lend themselves to inventive
        beauty.

The Playful Portrait of Life

The portrait of life –
a gathering of countless
glittering atom-like specks.

If one speck disappears in one direction
another finds a niche elsewhere.
The captivating image can become ugly
and lose all its charm.

The touch of one speck can fulfill a life.
Erase one line and a paradise blooms.
Beyond one word lies heaven,
beyond another word lies hell.

This portrait glitters like mica.
Life has a playful beauty –
move to the left and it changes shape,
move to the right and it shows another face.
Its beauty is in the eye of the beholder.
A discerning gaze will find Spring
even in the middle of Autumn.
Life's portrait is infinite.

Moments

1

The holy man's preaching urged generous donations.
He returned to his temple with a million dollars.

2

The guy returning from abroad had failed eighth grade
but took back with him a college graduate wife.

3

With birthing, care-giving, cooking, going to work
my days of sound sleep are gone.

4

I earn now as you do.
Why would you treat me like an old shoe?

5

To hell with Canada, my friend!
What happened to that promised diamond necklace?

6

Why would you have such desire for necklaces
when you are beautiful like the spring?

7

You roar like the monsoon thunder.
Come, let us embrace and cool down together

8

Your youth is hot like fire.
Why then are you cold like a marble slab to me?

9
Why can you never get enough gold,
my pearl-like beauty?

10
With false prophets everywhere,
to how many should I bow my head?

11
Their hearts overflow with lust and greed
but they continue their charade of chanting.

12
My girl is a bundle of soft silk.
Why would I worship stone idols?

13
He invites his girlfriends for drinks
and bills five hundred bucks to the government.

14
Politicians cut deals to gain power
but they keep telling us to join protest marches.

15
The same people who suffered in prisons for freedom
now rot again in jails.

16
Those who licked the shoes of colonizers
are now ministers wearing home-spun *khadi*

17

Complaining of her poor dowry, he killed the daughter-in-law.
But he prays to God for his daughter's welfare.

18

He killed the daughter after intercepting her lover's letter.
But he seeks a new bed every day.

19

Let your poetry manuscripts burn in fire!
Every weekend I spend lonesome nights.

khadi: coarse, home-spun cotton cloth worn by India's politicians as mere symbolic
homage to M.K. Gandhi, who used *khadi* during India's freedom movement to
boycott foreign goods and promote self-reliance.

Faith

I seem to have reached
the destination I looked for,
rough journey come to an end –
but every Eve sets to swinging
a lush spear of grain
that sends an Adam to a new world.

Praise Eve
with her swaying seed –
without her, my goal would have walled me,
ideals of freedom frozen to creed,
every question a heresy.

Now I am surrounded by faiths clamoring,
each one spreading its velvet path.
I have a stinging suspicion
that under the soft green
hide poisonous thorns –
but sharper is my nagging feeling
that even this new paradise will not escape
doctrine's viper strike.

Translated by Amritjit Singh and Wendy Barker

Prophet

From the outset religion has caused carnage in the world,
much blood shed in its name.

Every new prophet was a rebel against orthodoxy.
The faithful called him an infidel.
He came into the world, labored, and disappeared
as a new faith was born,
another rift etched into hearts,
another schism cut in.

Yet another came along to settle feuds and declared:
Think! Blood is life. Let your obsessions fade.
The truth of the world is bigger than faith.
The search for God and wealth is rope for the same trap.
If you want to fly high, sever the rope and escape the trap.

Fearless revolutionaries cut their way out,
flew up and surveyed the scene:
The learned man, the liberator of yesterday, is today's ruler
waving at the crowds.
His statue is anointed with others' blood
and he beams a false smile.

My Wool

All this fuss is not about laying into faith.
It is really about my wool.
The only question is –
Who among them will shear my wool?

The sharp-tongued clippers dance all around me,
closing in on me with their baskets of greed.
The baskets overflow but these gluttons are insatiable.

These shears, ever greedy for my fleece,
are eyeing my blood and meat too.

Instead of being a sacrificial lamb to these demagogues,
I think I had better get wise to their game.
Let me kill the sheep in me,
and rise as a lion to confront these shrill clippers.
Whoever heard of a lion being sheared?

The Moment of Creation

The fateful timing when word and idea embrace –
glimpsed, one instant,
gone, the next –
teases the mind with many faces, dances –

one minute Krishna romps with his beloved *gopi*s,
the next declares "I am God," and kisses the gallows.

The rough path from ecstasy to execution
stretches in one step the beginning and the end.

A gem is lost in the wilderness –
a crackling of prophets and voices.
I even set my self aside
as I meet the moment of creation.

Translated by Amritjit Singh and Wendy Barker

---

*gopi*s, literally "cowherd girls" in Sanskrit, invokes the unconditional love and
devotion to Krishna of his numerous female companions.

Dividing Line

Once you and I were one.
Time's blunt knife
has etched a line in our chests.
But what do ordinary people care about borders?
It's only politicians who find a use for boundaries.

Our clothes and patched blankets are torn into shreds.
Let us sit somewhere in the shade and mend them.
Let us break bread together.

ਲਕੀਰ

ਅਸਲ ਵਿਚ ਤਾਂ ਮੈਂ ਤੇ ਤੂੰ ਇੱਕੋ ਹੀ ਸਾਂ
ਸਮੇ ਦੀ ਖੁੰਢੀ ਛੁਰੀ ਨੇ
ਹਿੱਕੜੀ ਸਾਡੀ ਤੇ ਪਾ ਦਿਤੀ ਲਕੀਰ
ਪਰ ਫਕੀਰਾਂ ਦਾ ਲਕੀਰਾਂ ਨਾਲ਼ ਕੀ ਹੈ ਵਾਸਤਾ
ਇਹ ਵਜ਼ੀਰਾਂ ਦੇ ਹੀ ਨੇ ਕੰਮ ਆਉਂਦੀਆਂ।

ਗੋਦੜੀ ਸਾਡੀ ਦੇ ਉੱਡਦੇ ਨੇ ਲੰਗਾਰ
ਆ ਕਿ ਛਾਵੇਂ ਬੈਠ ਟਾਕੀ ਲਾਈਏ
ਰਲ਼ ਕੇ ਰੋਟੀ ਖਾਈਏ।

رل کے روٹی کھائیے

اصل وچ تاں مَیں تے تُوں اِکّو ای ساں
سمیں دی کھُنڈی چھُری نے
ہِکّڑی ساڈی تے پا دِتی لیکر
پر فقیراں دا لیکراں نال کی ہے واسطا
ایہہ وزیراں دے ہی نیں کم آوَندیاں

گودڑی ساڈی دے اُڈدے نیں لنگار
آ کہ چھاویں بیٹھ ٹاکی لائے
رل کے روٹی کھائیے

About the translators

AMRITJIT SINGH, Langston Hughes Professor of English at Ohio University, is a freelance writer, editor, translator, and book reviewer. He has authored and co-edited well over a dozen books, including *The Novels of the Harlem Renaissance*, *Indian Literature in English, 1827-1979: An Information Guide*, *India: An Anthology of Contemporary Writing*, *Conversations with Ralph Ellison*, *Postcolonial Theory and the United States*, *The Collected Writings of Wallace Thurman*, and *Interviews with Edward W. Said*.

JUDY RAY grew up on a farm in Sussex, England, and has lived in Uganda, India, Australia, and New Zealand. Currently she lives in Tucson, Arizona, where she is a volunteer ESL teacher. Her latest book of poetry is *To Fly Without Wings*, and her previous works include *Fishing in Green Waters*, *Pebble Rings*, *Pigeons in the Chandeliers*, and *The Jaipur Sketchbook*. With poet David Ray, she has edited *Fathers: A Collection of Poems* (St. Martin's, 1997).

WENDY BARKER teaches at the University of Texas at San Antonio. Her poetry collections and chapbooks include *Poems from Paradise*, *Ways of Whiteness*, *Let the Ice Speak*, *Winter Chickens*, *Eve Remembers*, and *Between Frames*. Her other books include *Rabindranath Tagore: Final Poems* (translated with Saranindranath Tagore), *Lunacy of Light: Emily Dickinson and the Experience of Metaphor*, and *The House is Made of Poetry: The Art of Ruth Stone* (co-edited with Sandra M. Gilbert).

GEORGIA SCOTT is the author of two books of poetry: *The Good Wife* and *The Penny Bride*, and a co-editor and co-translator of the anthology, *Dreams of Fires: 100 Polish Poems 1970-1989* – all published by Poetry Salzburg in Austria. She was born in Boston and lives in Poland.

About the poet

GURCHARAN RAMPURI (born 1929) has been writing poetry in Punjabi for six decades. Author of ten volumes of poetry, he moved to Vancouver, British Columbia, in 1964. He has won many awards, and his poems have been translated into many languages, including Russian, Hindi, Gujarati, and English. His *Collected Poems* appeared in India in 2001. Many of his lyrical poems have been set to music and sung by well-known singers such as Surinder Kaur and Jagjit Zirvi. He has won numerous awards in both India and Canada, including the 2007 Lifetime Achievement Award from the Punjabi Writers Forum of Vancouver, as well as the 2009 Achievement Award for Contributions to Punjabi Literature from the University of British Columbia.